CRACKING THE LOVE CODE

UNVEILING THE LESSONS OF RELATIONSHIP MISHAPS

VETA NEWTON

Quantity sales and special discounts are available on quantity purchases by corporations, associations, and others. For details, contact the publisher at the address above.

Orders by U.S. trade bookstores and wholesalers. Email info@ BeyondPublishing.net

The Beyond Publishing Speakers Bureau can bring authors to your live event. For more information or to book an event contact the Beyond Publishing Speakers Bureau speak@BeyondPublishing.net

The Author can be reached directly at BeyondPublishing.net

Manufactured and printed in the United States of America distributed globally by BeyondPublishing.net

BEYOND
PUBLISHING

New York | Los Angeles | London | Sydney

ISBN Hardcover: 978-1-63792-615-4
ISBN Softcover: 978-1-63792-616-1

CONTENTS

ACKNOWLEDGEMENTS

With Special Thanks:

"Cracking the Love Code: Lessons Learned from My Relationship Mishaps" has been a deeply fulfilling and transformative journey, one that would not have been possible without the grace and blessings of the Almighty.

In this heartfelt acknowledgment, I express my sincere gratitude to God for bestowing upon me the freedom of choice, allowing me to embark on a path that has touched the lives of many women of faith over 40.

First and foremost, I extend my utmost thanks to the Divine Creator for granting me the wisdom and resilience to navigate through my own relationship mishaps.

It is through these experiences, often challenging and arduous, that I gained the insight and understanding to guide others on their journeys of self-discovery and love.

To all the remarkable women of faith over 40 who have graced my life, from my mother , sisters, aunts, cousins, friends.

A special love for my friends Ron and Vonna Newton , this book would be an empty canvas without your courage and vulnerability to show me how worthy and valuable I am. Your words and love and true friendship was my inspiration to examine myself.

To Mary O'Conner. Thank you for diligently telling me to look at all I truly have to offer someone, and how deserving I am.

I am indebted to my family and friends who provided unwavering support and encouragement throughout this writing process. Your belief in my vision and unwavering love have been my anchor during moments of doubt and fatigue.

I extend my sincere appreciation to my editor and the entire publishing team, Beyond Publishing , whose dedication and expertise have polished this book into its best possible form. Your commitment to excellence has been instrumental in bringing my words to life.

To my readers, who are about to embark on a journey of self-discovery and empowerment, I am truly honored that you have chosen "Cracking the Love Code" as your guide.

May the lessons shared within these pages resonate with your hearts and lead you to more fulfilled relationships and a profound love for yourselves.

Finally, I offer my deepest gratitude to God once again. Your divine guidance has been a guiding light throughout this project, and I trust that your presence will continue to illuminate the paths of all those who seek love, understanding, and personal growth.

With love and humility,
Veta Newton

CRACKING THE LOVE CODE

UNVEILING THE LESSONS OF RELATIONSHIP MISHAPS

As far back as I can remember, I have always felt God's presence. Somehow in every event of my life, good or bad, there has been divine presence.

Let's be honest, we've all experienced disappointments, pain, grief, heartbreak, and loss. It's the take aways from these experiences that matter. How we handle our emotions and what we learn about ourselves is the true lessons.

What did we learn from these experiences, from the relationships? Most importantly, what did we discover about ourselves?

Did we allow certain behaviors, or fail to set boundaries, perhaps overlook our own needs in the pursuit of what we believed to be love?

CHAPTER 1

Discovering Your
True Self

Through my 66 years and numerous failed relationships, I've come to realize that the most crucial relationship in life is the one with yourself.

You teach others how you wish to be treated, loved and the boundaries and limits you've set.

I thank you for allowing me to share what I've experienced, what and how to express your desires and intentions.

Although there may not be one single "right" person out there, it may involve multiple connections, each offering lessons to help you grow and move toward what you truly desire.

Experiencing multiple failed relationships and the accompanying heartbreak can be emotionally challenging.

However, there are several valuable lessons that can be drawn from these difficult situations:

Self-reflection and personal growth

Failed relationships offer an opportunity for introspection. Take the time to analyze your past actions, behaviors, and relationship patterns.

Identify negative traits or patterns or traits that may have contributed to the difficulties faced. Use this self-awareness to facilitate personal growth and make positive changes for future relationships.

Clarifying your needs and values

Each failed relationship can help you gain a clearer understanding of your own needs, values, and priorities in a partnership. Reflect on what you truly desire in a relationship and what is important to you in terms of compatibility, communication, and emotional support. This knowledge can guide you toward healthier, more fulfilling connections in the future.

Establishing boundaries and self-care

Heartbreak often reveals the importance of setting boundaries and practicing self-care. Understand your own emotional limits, and learn to communicate your needs effectively within a relationship. Recognize when a relationship is no longer healthy for you and be prepared to walk away if necessary. Prioritize self-care by engaging in activities that promote your well-being, such as hobbies, exercise, or spending time with loved ones.

Patience and timing

Failed relationships can teach that timing and compatibility are crucial factors. Finding someone who aligns with your values, goals, and desires may take time. Understand that not every relationship will be the right fit, and exercise patience in your quest for a compatible partner. Rushing into relationships without ensuring compatibility can increase the likelihood of heartbreak.

Resilience and learning from mistakes

Heartbreak can be a catalyst for developing resilience and learning from past mistakes. Each failed relationship can provide valuable insights and lessons that contribute to personal growth and the ability to make better choices in the future.

Embrace these experiences as opportunities for growth rather than allowing them to discourage you.

Remember, everyone's journey is unique, and there is no predetermined timeline for finding a successful and fulfilling relationship. By reflecting on your experiences, learning from them, and working on personal growth, you can increase your chances of forming healthier connections and finding lasting happiness in future relationships.

Not every relationship that didn't work out is a failure. They are gifts and experiences that can lead to personal growth even in moments of discomfort and heartbreak.

Like attracts like, so the more positive you are and the more love you give yourself, the more likely you are to attract similar people. Your energy and vibe will align with your level of growth.

The way you speak to yourself matters! Is it negative or uplifting?

The Scars of Love -
A Japanese Analogy

The Scars of Love: A Kintsugi Analogy

This analogy holds a profound significance for me as it reshapes my perspective on failures. Everyone encounters setbacks, yet it is our outlook that enriches us.

My fascination with diverse cultures and their appreciation for life, particularly their commitment to simplicity, has led me to the Japanese art of Kintsugi.

In this practice, broken pottery is meticulously reassembled using lacquer mixed with gold, silver, or platinum, serving as a metaphor for embracing our flaws and imperfections.

It suggests that our full potential might remain unrealized until we experience profound pain or heartbreak.

This process doesn't merely restore the pottery; it elevates its value beyond its original form.

The gold used to repair the vessel symbolizes the price paid to piece ourselves back together. The scars persist, but like the way Jesus's scars shine outward for the world to see, they become a testament to our strength and resilience.

Kintsugi emphasizes not concealing our flaws but drawing attention to them, turning them into points of beauty and uniqueness.

The philosophy behind Kintsugi is rooted in the idea that flaws or cracks in an object should be embraced and highlighted as part of its history.

Similarly, healing from the pain of heartbreak can be seen as a process of emotional repair and growth.

Now, let's draw a comparison between Kintsugi and the journey of healing from heartbreak:

This technique focuses on not trying to hide our flaws, but draws attention to them.

Kintsugi is a traditional Japanese art form that involves repairing broken pottery using lacquer mixed with gold, silver, or platinum. The philosophy behind

Kintsugi is based on the idea that rather than hiding the flaws or cracks in an object, they should be embraced and highlighted as part of its history. Similarly, healing from the pain of heartbreak can be seen as a process of emotional repair and growth.

Here's a comparison between Kintsugi and healing from heartbreak:

Acknowledging the Brokenness:
Both Kintsugi and the process of healing from heartbreak commence with acknowledging the brokenness.
In Kintsugi, the broken pottery is not discarded or deemed worthless; instead, the broken pieces are collected and valued. Similarly, in healing from heartbreak, acknowledging the pain and accepting that the relationship is broken is the first step towards healing.

Embracing Imperfections:
Kintsugi celebrates the cracks and imperfections by filling them with precious metals, creating beautiful patterns.
Similarly, when healing from heartbreak, embracing your emotional scars and recognizing that they are part of your journey can lead to personal growth and resilience. Accepting that heartbreak is a natural part of life helps in moving forward.

Finding Beauty in the Flaws:
The mended pottery in Kintsugi becomes even more beautiful with the addition of gold or other metals. This transformation highlights the history and unique character of the object. Similarly, healing from heartbreak can lead to personal growth and self-discovery. Through the process of healing, individuals can find strength, wisdom, and new perspectives that add to their personal beauty.

Taking Time and Patience:

Kintsugi is a meticulous process that demands time, patience, and careful craftsmanship. Similarly, healing from heartbreak is a journey that takes time. It involves self-reflection, self-care, and allowing yourself to grieve and heal at your own pace. Just as Kintsugi cannot be rushed, the healing process from heartbreak requires patience and self-compassion.

This analogy beautifully captures the transformative nature of healing and personal growth, turning moments of heartbreak into opportunities for greater self-discovery and strength. It encourages a positive perspective on challenges and emphasizes the beauty that can emerge from embracing one's imperfections.

CHAPTER 3

Creating a
New Narrative

Kintsugi transforms broken pottery into a new piece with its own unique story. Similarly, healing from heartbreak involves creating a new narrative for yourself. It's an opportunity to redefine who you are, your values, and your goals. By learning from past experiences, you can build a stronger and more resilient version of yourself.

Both Kintsugi and the process of healing from heartbreak teach us that brokenness does not signify worthlessness. They remind us that healing and growth can arise from embracing our flaws and turning our pain into something beautiful and meaningful.

It can also teach each of us by accepting others, for their uniqueness and differences. Some of us are carrying more experiences and scars than others, which means using more gold to repair. This process makes us even more beautiful and valuable.

So once we have gone through pain and kept the right mindset, you will have become much more valuable, strong, self aware, and proud of your journey.

It takes courage to actually sit down with yourself and accept your faults without judgment and embrace your imperfections.

Whether you're grappling with a heart break or a job loss or a significant disappointment, we must remember that your scars are an integral part of you. They shape character, teach us and help us grow.

Heartbreak can be one of the most painful experiences we have in life, but it can also be the most liberating. It can be a chance to develop self discovery and an opportunity for growth.

In fact, its often the most difficult moments that teach us the most about ourselves and what we truly want out of life. While it may not seen apparent in the moment the pain from heartbreak can ultimately lead to a sense of joy and a profound appreciation for life.

Just like the scars of Jesus, they symbolize the love within each of us. They represent the sacrifices made for love, the true essence of love, and the risks we take in pursuit of it.

Heartbreak, while one of life's most painful experiences, can also be profoundly liberating.

It can provide an opportunity for self-discovery and personal growth. In fact, the most challenging moments often teach us the most about ourselves and our true desires in life.

It's an opportunity to redefine your identity, values, and goals. By learning from past experiences, you can construct a stronger, more resilient version of yourself.

Both Kintsugi and the process of healing from heartbreak teach us that brokenness does not signify worthlessness. They remind us that healing and growth can arise from embracing our imperfections and turning our pain into something beautiful and meaningful.

Moreover, they impart a valuable lesson in accepting others for their uniqueness and differences. Some of us carry more experiences and scars than others, which may require more "gold" to mend. This process makes us even more beautiful and valuable.

Once you've traversed pain with the right mindset, you emerge as someone more valuable, strong, self-aware, and proud of your journey.

Finding the ideal partner involves a combination of self-awareness, clear communication, and a willingness to invest time and effort in building a healthy relationship.

Here are some tips to help you in your quest for an **ideal partner**:

Self-Reflection:

- Understand your own values, goals, and priorities. Knowing yourself is crucial in finding someone who aligns with your lifestyle and aspirations.
- Reflect on past relationships to identify patterns, lessons learned, and the qualities that are essential to your happiness.

Define Your Priorities:

- Clearly define your must-haves and deal-breakers. Consider factors like values, communication styles, lifestyle preferences, and long- term goals.
- Understand the difference between superficial preferences and core values.

Effective Communication:

- Be open and honest about your expectations, desires, and boundaries. Effective communication is key to building trust and understanding in a relationship.
- Listen actively to your potential partner, and be receptive to their needs and perspectives.

Shared Interests and Values:
- Look for someone who shares common interests and values. Shared activities and beliefs can create a strong foundation for a lasting connection.
- Discuss important topics early on to ensure compatibility in areas such as religion, family, and life goals.

Emotional Intelligence:
- Seek a partner with emotional intelligence – someone who is self-aware, empathetic, and capable of navigating and expressing emotions.
- Emotional intelligence contributes to effective communication, conflict resolution, and overall relationship satisfaction.

Healthy Communication and Conflict Resolution:
- Choose a partner with whom you can communicate openly and resolve conflicts in a healthy manner. A relationship without effective communication can face challenges.

Supportive Relationship Dynamics:
- Look for a partner who supports your personal growth and encourages your pursuits. A healthy relationship involves mutual support and respect.
- Avoid relationships with power imbalances, control issues, or unhealthy dynamics.

Take Your Time:
- Building a strong connection takes time. Allow the relationship to develop organically, and avoid rushing into commitments.

- Take the time to get to know your partner in various situations and settings..

Trust Your Instincts:
- Trust your gut feelings about the person. If something feels off or raises concerns, address them openly and honestly.
- Pay attention to red flags and don't dismiss your instincts.

Remember that finding the ideal partner is a journey, and it's okay to reassess and adjust your priorities along the way. Focus on building a relationship based on mutual respect, shared values, and genuine connection.

Don't Settle

Not settling in relationships is important for your long-term happiness and fulfillment.

Here are some tips to help you avoid settling:

Know Your Worth:
- Understand your own value and what you bring to a relationship. Recognize your strengths, qualities, and the love you deserve.

Define Your Standards:
- Clearly define your standards and expectations for a relationship. Identify what is non-negotiable for you in terms of values, communication, and compatibility.

Identify Deal-Breakers:
- Determine your deal-breakers – the qualities or behaviors that you cannot accept in a partner. Be firm about not compromising on these essential aspects.

Prioritize Core Values:

- Focus on shared core values rather than superficial qualities. Shared values create a strong foundation for a lasting and meaningful connection.

Don't Settle for Comfort:

- Avoid staying in a relationship simply because it's comfortable or familiar. True growth and happiness often come from stepping out of your comfort zone.

Trust Your Instincts:

- Listen to your instincts and intuition. If something doesn't feel right or align with your goals, it's essential to address it rather than dismissing your feelings.

Be Patient:

- Patience is crucial in finding the right partner. Avoid rushing into a relationship or settling for someone who doesn't meet your standards out of fear of being alone.

Communicate Openly:

- Practice open and honest communication about your needs, desires, and expectations. Encourage your partner to do the same to ensure mutual understanding.

Seek Compatibility:

- Look for compatibility beyond surface-level qualities. Ensure alignment in areas such as life goals, communication styles, and long-term visions.

Maintain Independence:

- Maintain your independence and individual identity within the relationship. Avoid settling for a relationship that compromises your personal growth and well-being.

Learn from Past Mistakes:

- Reflect on past relationships and learn from any patterns or mistakes. Use these experiences to refine your understanding of what you truly need in a partner.

Be Open to Growth:

- Choose a partner who encourages personal growth and supports your aspirations. Avoid settling for someone who hinders your potential or limits your ambitions.

Don't Ignore Red Flags:

- Pay attention to red flags or warning signs. Address issues as they arise rather than ignoring them, hoping they will improve over time.

Build Self-Confidence:

- Cultivate self-confidence and a positive self-image. When you value yourself, you are less likely to settle for a relationship that doesn't meet your standards.

Remember that a healthy, fulfilling relationship is built on mutual respect, shared values, and a deep connection.

Don't compromise on what truly matters to you, and trust that the right partner will align with your expectations.

CHAPTER 5

The Physical Pains
of Heartbreak

Describing the literal and physical pain of a heartbreak can be a deeply personal and subjective experience, as it can vary from person to person. However, here are some common ways people may describe the emotional and physical aspects of heartbreak:

1 Emotional Pain:

- Overwhelming sadness: It feels like an immense weight on your chest, a constant ache in your heart, and an emotional heaviness that consumes you.

- Deep Sorrow: It's like a persistent feeling of emptiness, as if a part of you is missing or has been torn away.

- Intense grief: It can feel like waves of sadness crashing over you, leaving you feeling shattered and emotionally fragile.

- Emotional numbness: You may feel a sense of detachment from the world and find it difficult to experience joy or engage in activities you once enjoyed.

2 Physical Sensations:

- Tightness in the chest: Many people describe a sensation of tightness or heaviness in the chest, almost as if someone is squeezing or constricting their heart.

- Stomachaches or loss of appetite: Heartbreak can lead to a loss of appetite or a constant feeling of butterflies or knots in the stomach.
- Exhaustion and lack of energy: The emotional distress caused by heartbreak can result in physical fatigue, making it challenging to concentrate or engage in daily activities.
- Insomnia or disrupted sleep patterns: Difficulty falling asleep or frequent waking during the night are common experiences, as the mind often races with thoughts and memories of the lost relationship.

3 *Overall Experience:*

- Aching and throbbing pain: Heartbreak can feel like a physical ache or throbbing sensation, almost as if the heart itself is in pain.
- Breathlessness or shortness of breath: It may feel like it's hard to catch your breath, as if the air around you is thin or suffocating.
- Sensitivity to triggers: Even seemingly insignificant reminders of the lost relationship, such as a song or a familiar scent, can trigger intense emotional and physical reactions.

It's important to remember, everyone experiences and copes with heartbreak differently.

While these descriptions may resonate with some, they may not capture the full range of emotions and physical sensations felt by others. It's important to acknowledge and respect the individuality of each person's experience. If you or someone you know is struggling with heartbreak, seeking support from loved ones, friends, or professionals can be beneficial.

Furthermore, heartbreak can also teach us important lessons about our own needs and boundaries. Reflecting on what went wrong in a past relationship, we can gain insight into what we need and want in a future partner.

Learn to set boundaries and communicate our needs more effectively , can lead to more fulfilling relationships in the long run.

After heartbreak or loss, is the opportunity for emotional release. When we allow ourselves to fully feel and process the pain of breakup, we can experience a sense of catharsis and clarity. The emotional release can be incredibly freeing and allow us to move on with greater sense of peace and acceptance.

After a breakup or loss, we can focus on our own needs and desires rather than solely of others.

I'm in the midst of discovering that experiences are placed in life for growth, to catapult, and awaken our deeper selfs. Be it made by choice or happenstance.

Pain and heartbreak is part of living. The sooner we realize and accept this, will help us not wonder why something unfortunate happened to us?

CHAPTER 6

Gratitude and Joy

Embracing a joyful, positive and upbeat outlook can transformative in various aspects of life.

Here are benefits of maintaining a joyful and gracious attitude.

1 Improve overall well-being:

A joyful attitude, is linked to experiencing positive emotions which can significantly boost your immune system. And mental health. It can boost your immune system, lower stress levels, and improve your overall well- being.

2 Enhance relationships:

A joyful disposition contributes to being pleasant and engaging in social situations, which can foster stronger relationships, People are naturally attracted to those who are positive and joyful, and they are more likely to want to spend time with you.

3 Increases productivity:

Joyful individuals tend to be more motivated and energized, which can increase your productivity. Joyful people tend to be more creative, innovative, and persistent, which can help them achieve their goals more easily.

4 Aids in coping:

Cultivating a joyful attitude, equips individuals to better handle stress and adversity. Joyful people demonstrate resilience and optimism empowering them to navigating difficult situations.

Being joyful, positive and upbeat changes everything.

The biblical perspective encourages counting it all joy in the face of trials (James 1:2-4), emphasizing that challenges can produce patience, endurance, and a stronger faith.

Maintaining joy, even amid sorrow, is emphasized through a powerful practice—praying for those who have caused hurt.

While it may sound unconventional, it involves releasing the person back to the universe, lifting them up in prayer, and speaking their name as you pray. This practice helps in preserving joy and authenticity in prayer, as God understands the hurt and the heart.

Reflections on Life and Relationships:

At 66, I find myself looking inward, perhaps prompted by a growing awareness of mortality or personal development.

A belief in a higher being, ingrained in my upbringing, provided a constant sense of a creator, protector, and lover of my soul.

Despite this knowledge, I didn't always tap into it when making life choices. The realization that there is someone who understands and loves me unconditionally was always present but not always applied.

My 25-year marriage taught me valuable lessons about priorities in relationships. Recognizing that each person should be a priority led to a mutual parting of ways when events and circumstances were beyond our control.

Enduring significant trauma prompted introspection, whether due to age or divine intervention seeking to teach profound lessons. The journey through online dating, initially daunting at my age, revealed the importance of trusting wisely and not ignoring instincts and intuition

Enduring trauma

Prompted introspection, whether due to age or divine intervention seeking to teach profound lessons.

The journey through online dating, initially daunting at my age, revealed the importance of trusting wisely and not ignoring instincts and intuition.

I learned that what I want in my next relationship, is to be a priority, just as I give them priority. Each should be #1 in the relationship, and if that changes or doesn't happen, you are not going to be fulfilled.

But sometimes, events and circumstances are out of our control and we eventually parted mutual ways I've endured much trauma in life

My most recent event was falling in love with someone online

Again , I'm not sure if its because of my age or because God is always wanting to teach us something, and sometimes, some of us need a REALLY big thing to shake our world , in order to get through to us. I listened to a relationship coach online , who said online dating really is the best way to meet your ideal partner.

But, I had no experience and this was really out of the realm I grew up.

Because of how I grew up, I really trusted easily. I wanted true love, a love like I had never experienced during all the other relationships.

Of the relationships I've had none were as painful as the most recent. But maybe it's my perspective. When I was younger I seemed to have gotten over things more easily and quicker .

My first experience with online dating was very daunting, especially at my age. I was told that online was the most successful way to meet and engaged with others. I always thought that I would meet the usual way, through friends, work or out of the "clear blue sky," as George sings. ha

Long story, short, I found myself being sucked into the abyss , believing words instead of actions. Believing what one told me, versus the fruit from those words.

The practice of giving someone the benefit of the doubt involves assuming good intentions despite evidence to the contrary.

This concept necessitates weighing the potential benefits and risks. Instincts and gut feelings should be trusted to guide decisions regarding trust.

So what does giving someone the benefit of the doubt mean actually? There are pros and cons to giving the "benefit of the doubt"

Giving someone the benefit of the doubt means that you are choosing to believe that a person's intentions or actions are good, even if there is some evidence to suggest otherwise.

The journey involves feeling and processing emotions rather than seeking replacements to heal unaddressed wounds. Placing boundaries and limits becomes a path to newfound peace, especially in the unfamiliar territory of online dating.

Understanding the importance of getting to know someone beyond constant texting, interpreting non-verbal cues, and setting boundaries aligns with the pursuit of inner peace.

Recognizing that placing a value on life and establishing boundaries guard against toxic relationships is a fundamental step toward personal growth and contentment.

Benefit of the Doubt:

Pros and Cons

The practice of giving someone the benefit of the doubt involves assuming good intentions despite evidence to the contrary. While it can build trust and maintain relationships, it carries the risk of being taken advantage of, ignoring red flags, and feeling let down.

Understanding this concept necessitates weighing the potential benefits and risks. Instincts and gut feelings should be trusted to guide decisions regarding trust.

Here are some potential pros and cons of giving someone the benefit of the doubt

Pros and Cons of Giving Someone the Benefit of the Doubt: Pros:

Building Trust
- Giving someone the benefit of the doubt helps build trust between you and the other person. Assuming their good intentions demonstrates your willingness to trust them in future interactions.

Maintaining Relationships
- Choosing to give someone the benefit of the doubt contributes to maintaining relationships, especially with friends or family members. It also prevents misunderstandings or hurt feelings that may arise from assuming the worst.

Positive Attitude:
- Assuming the best in people cultivates a more positive attitude towards life and those around you. This mindset enables you to focus on the good in people and view situations in a more optimistic light.

Cons:

Being Taken Advantage Of:
- Giving someone the benefit of the doubt too often may lead to them taking advantage of your kindness. They might assume you will always believe them and may not feel compelled to act with integrity.

Ignoring Red Flags:
- Ignoring warning signs is a significant risk of giving someone the benefit of the doubt. This can result in overlooking indications that the person may not be trustworthy or has ulterior motives. It's crucial to be aware of these signs and use your judgment to assess trustworthiness.

Feeling Let Down:
- If you give someone the benefit of the doubt, and they ultimately act in a harmful or hurtful way, you may feel let down or

disappointed. This can lead to feelings of distrust or cynicism towards others in the future.

Overall Evaluation:

While there are potential benefits to giving someone the benefit of the doubt, there are also risks involved. It's crucial to weigh these factors carefully and use your best judgment when deciding whether or not to trust someone. Trusting your instincts or gut feelings can play a vital role in making the best decision for yourself. The key is to strike a balance between trust and vigilance, allowing for a healthy and discerning approach to relationships.

Ignoring red flags

This is a big one!

Giving someone the benefit of the doubt can cause you to ignore warning signs that could indicate that the person is not trustworthy or has ulterior motives. It's important to be aware of these signs and to use your judgement to determine whether or not the person is trustworthy.

CHAPTER 7

Knowing Your Value

The pivotal lesson learned involves knowing one's value. Analyzing personal wants and needs, recognizing red flags, and not succumbing to empty promises are crucial.

Actions speak louder than words, and identifying integrity, values, morals, and kindness in a person's actions establishes trustworthiness.

So this is my great lesson!! *Know your value.*

The journey involves feeling and processing emotions rather than seeking replacements to heal unaddressed wounds. Placing boundaries and limits becomes a path to newfound peace, especially in the unfamiliar territory of online dating.

Understanding the importance of getting to know someone beyond constant texting, interpreting non-verbal cues, and setting boundaries aligns with the pursuit of inner peace. Recognizing that placing a value on life and establishing boundaries guard against toxic relationships is a fundamental step toward personal growth and contentment.

Don't waste time listening to empty promises and words.

I want to teach woman how to know their value and self worth.

Encourage Self-Reflection:

- Help explore her values, goals, and aspirations. Understanding oneself is the foundation of self-worth.

Promote Self-Love:

- Emphasize the importance of self-love and self-care. Encourage activities that bring her joy and fulfillment.

Highlight Strengths and Achievements:

- Remind of her strengths and past achievements. Building on positive aspects of her identity boosts self-esteem.

Discuss Healthy Relationships:

- Have open conversations about what constitutes a healthy relationship. Discuss mutual respect, communication, and support.

Educate on Boundaries:

- Teach about personal boundaries and their significance. Emphasize that setting and enforcing boundaries is a healthy and necessary aspect of relationships.

Identify Warning Signs:

- Help recognize red flags in relationships, such as manipulation, disrespect, or control. Awareness is crucial for maintaining healthy boundaries.

Encourage Communication Skills:

- Foster effective communication skills. Help her express her needs, concerns, and feelings assertively but respectfully.

Establish a Support System:
- Encourage to surround herself with supportive friends and family who uplift and respect her.

Teach Decision-Making Skills:
- Assist in developing decision-making skills. Knowing when to say no and making choices aligned with her values is empowering.

Provide Resources:
- Share books, articles, or workshops on self-improvement, self-esteem, and healthy relationships.

Role Modeling:
- Demonstrate healthy boundaries and self-respect in your own life. Lead by example.

Empower Financial Independence:
- Advocate for financial independence. Having control over her finances contributes to overall independence.

Offer Professional Support:
- If necessary, suggest seeking therapy or counseling to explore deeper issues and develop coping mechanisms.

Celebrate Progress:
- Acknowledge and celebrate small victories. Positive reinforcement boosts confidence and motivates further growth.

Remember that empowering someone to value themselves and establish healthy boundaries is an ongoing process. Patience, understanding, and consistent support are key elements in this journey.

CHAPTER 8

Finding Trust in Actions, Not Words

When someone endlessly talks and makes promises without backing them up with actions, resist getting lured into the fantasy. Words, as you know, can be cheap.

The real measure lies in the fruit of their words— their actions. If actions are absent, it's time to walk away swiftly and shut it down.

As the body without the spirit is dead, so is faith without deeds dead.

It's easy to fall prey to someone who spins flattering words. Avoid wasting time on empty promises and words.

Actions reveal true character, while words often unveil only a façade. Don't be swayed by sweet talk; anyone can say anything.

A trustworthy person is one whose actions speak louder than words, someone who does what they say they will do.

Such an individual embodies integrity, values, morals, and genuine kindness.

Learning to acknowledge and process your feelings is crucial. Acting like nothing happened might seem like a way to move on, but it often leaves you searching for external sources to heal what you haven't addressed within yourself.

Failure to place value on your own life and set boundaries can lead to giving yourself to individuals with malicious intent and narcissistic behaviors. This pattern fosters misery and allows the venom injected by others to fester within.

Discovering peace comes with learning to establish boundaries and limits. In the uncharted territory of online dating, it's vital to get to know someone beyond constant texting. Texting, for me, is not the ideal mode of communication. It leaves too much room for misinterpretation without the benefit of eye contact or body language. Perhaps, I'm just not cut out for it, and honestly, I don't think I want to be.

CHAPTER 9

Setting Boundaries for Safe Online Dating

Online dating presents numerous opportunities but demands careful boundaries for safety and well-being. Consider the following guidelines:

Limit Personal Information:
- Protect your personal information by refraining from sharing your full name, home address, or identifying details until trust is established.

Cautious In-Person Meetings:
- Opt for public places when meeting someone in person for the first few times. Inform a trusted person of your whereabouts and the person you're meeting.

Avoid Intimate Photo Sharing:
- Refrain from sharing intimate photos or videos online to prevent potential misuse or harm.

Communication Boundaries:

- Clearly define how often you want to communicate and when you're available to talk. Resist the pressure to respond immediately to every message.

Trust Your Instincts:

- If something feels off or uncomfortable, trust your instincts. Prioritize your safety and well-being.

The Pros of
Online Dating

Online dating offers various advantages:

Increased Access:

- Expands your dating pool, providing access to a diverse range of potential partners beyond immediate social circles.

Convenience:

- Allows connection with potential partners at any time and from anywhere, catering to individuals with busy schedules.

Matching Algorithms:

- Utilizes sophisticated algorithms to match individuals based on interests, values, and preferences, streamlining the initial screening process.

Communication Opportunities:

- Provides diverse communication options, fostering connections through messaging, video chats, or emails before in-person meetings.

Specific Preferences:

- Allows filtering based on specific criteria, such as age, location, interests, and values, increasing the likelihood of finding compatible matches.

Overcoming Shyness:

- Offers a more comfortable platform for individuals with social anxiety, allowing them to initiate conversations without immediate face-to- face pressure.

Self-Discovery:

- Facilitates self-discovery by helping individuals understand their preferences, values, and relationship needs through interactions and experiences.

Diverse Interactions:

- Exposes individuals to a diverse range of people, broadening perspectives and increasing cultural understanding.

Despite these advantages, caution is necessary.

Best practices for online safety should always be followed to mitigate potential risks.

Verifying Legitimacy:

Assessing the legitimacy of an online connection involves specific steps:

Research Online Presence:

- Conduct a thorough online search of their name and shared photos, checking for inconsistencies or red flags.

Verify Information:

- Cross-check details provided by the person, such as occupation or education, to identify any discrepancies.

Watch for Relationship Rush:

- Be cautious of accelerated relationships or professions of love too soon, as scammers often use emotional manipulation.

Avoid Sharing Sensitive Information:

- Never share personal or financial information without verifying the person's identity to prevent potential scams.

Additional Advice for Online Dating:

Inappropriate Picture Requests:

- Refuse inappropriate picture requests. If someone delays asking for a date for an extended period, consider moving on.

Video Call or In-Person Meeting:

- Request a video call or an in-person meeting to assess the person's authenticity.

Trust Your Instincts:

- Pay attention to your gut feelings and exercise caution if something feels off.

Seek External Input:

- Share concerns with trusted friends or family for additional perspectives and insights.

Online dating can be a positive experience when approached with caution and thoughtful boundaries.

Remember, these steps can help you evaluate the legitimacy of a person, but they do not guarantee certainty.

Scammers can be skilled at creating elaborate facades, so it's crucial to remain vigilant and prioritize your personal safety.

CHAPTER 11

Unveiling Online
Deception

My Personal Encounter and the Need for Awareness

In my quest for companionship, I unwittingly neglected safety precautions and dismissed my inner voice, leading me into a web of deceit that persisted for months.

The individual in question, whom I had been communicating with extensively, consistently postponed our planned meeting, citing last- minute business trips.

His claim that his company, a Bitcoin venture, was retaining him due to soaring interest in Miami raised my suspicions—the first red flag that I, regrettably, chose to overlook. Hindsight, as they say, is always 20/20.

In retrospect, I find myself extending the "benefit of the doubt" once again.

It took considerable time before the realization dawned upon me: this person was not legitimate, and his return was nothing more than a mirage. The experience left me with a deep desire to share my story, hoping to raise awareness about the various deceptive scenarios that individuals may encounter in the realm of online dating.

Reflecting on my past, it becomes evident that I've allowed instances of abusive behavior in the name of love, a vulnerability that predators often exploit. This brings me to the topic of narcissists—individuals who possess a particular set of traits that make them adept at manipulation.

I've encountered narcissists in my journey, drawn to them by my inclination to give the "benefit of the doubt."

Unfortunately, this tendency makes individuals like me susceptible to the subtle control tactics employed by narcissists, who expertly manipulate their subjects.

It's crucial to understand that narcissists seek specific qualities and traits in others to fulfill their needs and boost their self-esteem. It's not a one-size-fits-all situation, as people's behaviors and preferences are intricate and diverse.

Recognizing these patterns and being aware of the tactics employed by such individuals is vital for safeguarding oneself in the complex world of online interactions.

My journey serves as a cautionary tale, urging others to stay vigilant and informed, creating a shield against the potential pitfalls of online dating.

Another red flag is grammar. If you're texting and they use inappropriate grammar, or punctuation , you're possibly dealing with a scammer. But not always. Once you begin to communicate , you'll know straight up.

Grammar and accent can be potential red flags when getting involved with someone online for a few reasons:

Language proficiency: Poor grammar, frequent spelling mistakes, and inconsistent language usage may indicate that the person is not a native speaker of the language they are communicating in. While this alone doesn't necessarily mean someone is dishonest or malicious, it can raise concerns about their ability to effectively communicate and build a strong connection with you.

Identity verification: In some cases, scammers and individuals with ill intentions may pretend to be someone they are not. They might adopt a fake identity or use someone else's photos and personal information to create an online persona. Inconsistencies between their stated background or location and their grammar or accent could be an indication that they are not being truthful about who they are.

Cultural differences: Accents and language usage can reflect a person's cultural background. While it's important to be open-minded and embrace cultural diversity, significant discrepancies between a person's claimed background and their accent or grammar might warrant further investigation. It's possible that someone is intentionally misrepresenting themselves to gain trust or manipulate others.

Communication barriers: If there is a noticeable language barrier between you and the person you're interacting with, it can hinder effective communication and understanding. Miscommunication or misunderstandings due to language differences might lead to frustration, confusion, or conflicts in the relationship.

Consistency and authenticity: Authenticity is crucial in any online relationship. Inconsistencies in grammar or accent, especially when coupled with other suspicious behaviors, may raise doubts about the person's true intentions or the veracity of the information they provide. It's important to be cautious when encountering such inconsistencies.

While grammar and accent alone should not be the sole basis for judging someone's character or intentions, they can serve as warning signs when combined with other suspicious behaviors or inconsistencies. It's always advisable to exercise caution and use your judgment when engaging in online relationships, especially when personal information or emotions are involved.

They'll want you to get off the app straight away, and onto another chat app. Whats app is commonly used . If asked to move from the dating app to another form of communication be aware . The excuse is they want to use Whats App for personal use so he didn't have to use his work phone. Ok, that kind of made sense to me….? There goes me giving the benefit of the doubt again.

Love bombing right away is another flag to look for. You're so beautiful, I can see myself spending my life with you, so on and so on.

Narcissists may target individuals displaying codependent tendencies, prioritizing the narcissist's needs and struggling to set boundaries.

It's crucial to recognize that narcissists engage in manipulative and exploitative behaviors, making relationships with them emotionally draining and damaging.

Signs Associated with Narcissistic Personality

Traits

Narcissism, characterized by a grandiose sense of self-importance, excessive need for admiration, and lack of empathy, has associated signs and behaviors. While only a professional can diagnose Narcissistic Personality Disorder (NPD), common signs include:

Grandiosity: Exaggerated sense of self-importance, frequently boasting achievements and talents.

Need for Admiration: Excessive desire for praise, attention, and validation from others.

Lack of Empathy: Difficulty understanding and sharing others' feelings, showing insensitivity

Sense of Entitlement: Belief in deserving special treatment and privileges, expecting others to cater to their needs.

Exploitative Behavior: Exploiting others for personal gain using manipulation, deceit, or coercion without remorse.

Arrogance and Superiority: Displaying arrogance and a sense of superiority, looking down upon others.

Envy and Jealousy: Feeling intense envy, especially towards those perceived as more successful.

Lack of Accountability: Avoiding responsibility, shifting blame, and struggling with criticism or admitting mistakes.

Interpersonal Difficulties: Challenging relationships marked by conflicts and power struggles.

Fragile Self-esteem: Despite outward grandiosity, narcissists may have easily wounded self-esteem, reacting strongly to criticism or rejection.

These signs alone do not diagnose Narcissistic Personality Disorder; a qualified mental health professional is needed for an accurate assessment.

Ron and Vonna Newton, dear friends of mine, opened my eyes to the realization that I have much to offer, but lacked self-respect. They emphasized that recognizing my self-worth needs to begin with me.

Building self-esteem is a gradual process requiring self-reflection, self-care, and consistent effort.

Here are steps for those with low self-esteem to increase their chances of finding an ideal partner:

Practice Self-Compassion:

Treat yourself with kindness, challenge negative self-talk, and replace it with positive affirmations. Recognize everyone's strengths and weaknesses.

Set Realistic Goals:

Celebrate small accomplishments, focusing on personal growth rather than comparisons. Acknowledge your efforts and set achievable goals.

Identify Negative Beliefs:

Explore beliefs contributing to low self-esteem. Challenge and replace unworthy or inadequate thoughts with positive and realistic ones.

Cultivate Self-Care Habits:

Prioritize physical, emotional, and mental well-being. Engage in activities bringing joy, relaxation, and fulfillment. Embrace practices like exercise, proper nutrition, sufficient sleep, and hobbies.

Surround Yourself with Positivity:

Seek supportive people who uplift you. Avoid relationships or environments reinforcing negative self-perceptions. Build a network of those who appreciate and value you.

Focus on Personal Strengths:

Acknowledge your unique qualities, talents, and skills. Use them as a foundation for personal growth and engage in activities showcasing your abilities.

Practice Self-Acceptance:

Embrace yourself, strengths and weaknesses included. Understand imperfections make you unique. Acceptance is crucial for building self- esteem.

Seek Professional Support:

If self-esteem issues persist, seek guidance from therapists, counselors, or support groups to address underlying issues.

Common Traits That Narcissists Seek in Others:

Admiration and Validation:

Narcissists crave constant praise, attention, and recognition to boost their fragile self-esteem. They seek individuals willing to provide admiration and validation.

Submissiveness:

Narcissists prefer individuals who are submissive, compliant, and easily manipulated. They seek control and dislike challenges to their authority.

Empathy and Compassion:

Despite lacking genuine empathy, narcissists may target empathetic and compassionate individuals to exploit their kindness for personal benefit.

Idealization:

Narcissists look for individuals who idealize and idolize them, placing them on a pedestal. They desire to be seen as extraordinary in the eyes of others.

Enabling Behavior:

Narcissists are drawn to people who enable their tendencies, catering to their demands, overlooking faults, and making excuses for their behavior.

Codependency:

Remember, finding an ideal partner is not solely dependent on self- esteem, but valuing yourself positively impacts relationships. Embrace your worth, take steps towards personal growth, and be patient throughout the journey.

Learning to stop handing over my essence, being, and attributes to the unworthy was a crucial lesson for me.

Many women aim to please and nurture, wonderful qualities unless it nurtures pain. Ignoring red flags and giving our best to everyone, regardless of deserving it, must change.

Our qualities should be earned through communication and actions.

Thinking that tolerance, kindness, and patience will make others see your value is a common misconception. You shouldn't have to work hard for love. Your ideal partner will have the desired qualities, and the relationship will be natural and organic.

Learn to praise God when He removes someone or something from your life. Instead of feeling disappointment realize that God sees what you didn't see, and He heard things you didn't hear.

Stop the negative self-talk that sabotages and paralyzes, preventing you from moving forward and finding something better.

CHAPTER 13

What happens when
we self sabotage?

Self-sabotage refers to behaviors or thought patterns that harm oneself and interfere with achieving personal goals or fulfilling one's potential.

It can take many forms, such as procrastination, negative self-talk, avoidance, self-medication with drugs or alcohol, or engaging in destructive relationships or behaviors.

Self-sabotage often stems from underlying psychological issues, such as low self-esteem, fear of failure or success, self-doubt, or past traumas.

Identifying the root causes of self-sabotage can be helpful in addressing and overcoming these behaviors.

Self-sabotage is a common behavior where individuals undermine their own success, happiness, or well-being. Identifying the issues associated with self-sabotage is a crucial first step in breaking this pattern. Here's a guide on understanding and overcoming self-sabotage:

1 Identify Patterns and Triggers:
- Reflect on Past Behavior: Look back on situations where you sabotaged your own efforts. Identify patterns and commonalities.
- Recognize Triggers: Determine the situations, emotions, or thoughts that trigger self-sabotage. It could be fear of failure, fear of success, low self-esteem, or other emotional triggers.

2 Understand the Root Causes:
- Explore Your Beliefs: Examine your beliefs about yourself, success, and worthiness. Deep-rooted negative beliefs can fuel self- sabotage.
- Past Experiences: Reflect on past experiences or traumas that may have contributed to your current mindset.

3 Build Self-Awareness:
- Mindfulness and Reflection: Practice mindfulness to stay present and aware of your thoughts and actions. Regularly reflect on your feelings and behaviors.
- Journaling: Keep a journal to track your thoughts, emotions, and behaviors. This can help you detect patterns and gain insights.

4 Challenge Negative Self-Talk:
- Cognitive Restructuring: Replace negative thoughts with positive and realistic ones. Challenge irrational beliefs and replace them with affirmations.
- Self-Compassion: Treat yourself with kindness. Understand that everyone makes mistakes, and failure is a part of learning.

5 Set Realistic Goals:
- Break Down Goals: Set achievable, realistic goals. Break larger goals into smaller, manageable steps. Celebrate small victories

along the way.

- Focus on Progress: Shift your focus from perfection to progress. Embrace the learning process and growth.

6 Develop Healthy Coping Mechanisms:

- Stress Management: Learn healthy ways to cope with stress, anxiety, or overwhelming emotions. This might include exercise, meditation, or seeking support from friends and family.

- Seek Professional Help: Consider therapy or counseling to address deeper emotional issues and learn effective coping strategies.

7 Create a Support System:

- Surround Yourself with Positivity: Build a supportive network of friends, family, or mentors who encourage and uplift you.

- Accountability Partners: Share your goals with someone you trust who can hold you accountable.

8 Visualize Success:

- Visualization Techniques: Use visualization to imagine yourself succeeding. This can help shift your mindset and create a positive outlook.

- Affirmations: Repeat positive affirmations that reinforce your ability to succeed

9 Learn from Setbacks:

- Growth Mindset: Adept a growth mindset that sees setbacks as opportunities for learning and improvement.

- Adept and Adjust: When faced with challenges, adept your strategies and adjust your approach rather than succumbing to self- sabotage

10 Celebrate Achievements:

- Acknowledge Success: Celebrate your achievements, no matter how small. Positive reinforcement strengthens the motivation to continue moving forward.

Conclusion:

Overcoming self-sabotage is an ongoing process that requires self- awareness, self-compassion, and a commitment to personal growth. It's beneficial to seek professional guidance if deep-rooted issues persist.

Developing a positive mindset and healthy coping mechanisms can gradually break the cycle of self-sabotage.

To break the cycle of self-sabotage, it's important to cultivate self- awareness and self-compassion.

To break this cycle of self sabotage means acknowledging and accepting one's flaws and weaknesses without judgment or shame, and focusing on positive self-talk and self-care.

Setting realistic goals, breaking them down into manageable steps, and rewarding oneself for progress can also help build momentum and confidence.

Therapy and counseling can also be effective in addressing self-sabotage, as they provide a safe and supportive space to explore and work through underlying issues.

Evil has always existed, tracing back to the time of Adam and Eve.

However, in today's world, it has found numerous avenues to proliferate, becoming easily accessible.

I can speak on this matter from the perspective of my upbringing—a time characterized by innocence, joy, and the freedom to explore.

Going outside, playing with friends, and returning home before supper were routine activities, devoid of the fear of evil intentions or harm from others.

My family instilled in me the belief of treating others as I would want to be treated, following the golden rule.

This principle emphasizes extending the same kindness to others that you would desire for yourself, your mother, or any family member.

Imagine a world where everyone embraced this concept—what a wonderful thought.

Growing up with a belief in God is a positive influence, but the type of religious upbringing also plays a significant role. I was raised in a "spirit- filled" church that believed in practices like speaking in tongues and being slain in the spirit.

Alongside these spiritual experiences, there was a strong emphasis on the consequences of sin—a constant threat of hellfire and brimstone. The atmosphere instilled a sense of guilt for every perceived transgression, be it a bad thought, a spoken word, or an action that fell short of divine expectations.

Despite nurturing a lifelong dream of writing a book, I consistently dismissed the idea, erroneously believing that I lacked the intelligence or knowledge to start.

The problem lay in my self-deprecating thoughts. Instead of valuing myself and saying, "Yes, give it a try," I remained trapped in negative thinking.

Shifting my self-talk language became imperative—what if it does work out? No risk, no reward. Learning to push my mind beyond its perceived limits, embracing the unusual, and understanding that we can control our thoughts, as mentioned in the Bible.

Most of our thoughts are just that—thoughts. Allow them to exist and then let them depart. Keep your spiritual heart vigilant, as it is the command center of the soul, mind, spirit, and affections—springs of life flow from it.

I came across an article about a professor who assigned his students the task of writing a letter to their favorite authors, seeking advice on how to embark on their writing journey.

Out of all the students, only one author took the time to respond. The advice given was simple: start that very night and write a poem.

It wasn't meant for anyone else's eyes, just an exercise to put thoughts on paper. The next step? Tear it up and throw it away.

The profound lesson here is that you'll be rewarded. Through this act, you begin to experience becoming yourself, learning more about who you are, and nurturing the growth of your soul. It's a confidence-building exercise, a practice in the art of writing.

Taking this advice to heart, I poured out my pain and heartache onto paper, letting tears flow onto the pages below.

Reflecting on my many failed relationships, I recognized a pattern. I never paused to stop and reflect, to assess what I could glean from each situation. I hadn't taken the time to learn from my experiences and apply that wisdom to avoid repeating the same patterns.

In the past, I viewed my failures, heartbreaks, and stumbling blocks as punishments. Punishments for not taking the time to ponder my actions, resulting in the inevitable consequences.

It was a belief that I was being punished by God for not living the right way or doing the right things.

Recently, I've come to believe that God has already forgiven us—forgiven us for every sin committed and those we'll commit in the future. How freeing and liberating is that?

No longer burdened by the need to ask for forgiveness incessantly, I have realized that this is not the way God intends us to live. I've become more forgiving of myself and others.

Accepting that things won't always go as planned is a blessing. By limiting expectations, we reduce disappointments and learn to roll with the punches.

I'm starting to understand that we must be thankful for failures and setbacks. They are gifts that help us, teach us, and refine us—much like coal going through fire to emerge higher and shine brighter.

Our shine becomes a magnet, drawing blessings to us, blessings we can share with others.

The biggest obstacle? Getting out of your own head, overcoming overthinking, and seeing failures as opportunities for growth rather than the worst that could happen.

CHAPTER 14

Overthinking

Overthinking refers to the act of dwelling excessively on thoughts, analyzing situations, and creating hypothetical scenarios that often lead to increased stress and anxiety.

While thinking things through can be helpful in certain situations, overthinking can be detrimental to one's mental well-being and decision- making process. Here are some common pitfalls of overthinking and strategies to help stop it.

Overthinking can lead to a state of analysis paralysis, where you become stuck in an endless loop of thinking without taking any action.

This can hinder productivity and prevent you from making decisions. To overcome this, set clear deadlines for making decisions and take small steps forward, even if you're uncertain. Trust yourself and your ability to adapt if needed.

Overthinking often involves negative and self-critical thoughts, which can lower self-esteem and increase anxiety. Recognize when you're engaging in negative self-talk and challenge those thoughts by questioning their validity. Replace them with more positive and realistic affirmations.

Overthinking can lead to heightened stress and anxiety levels as your mind continuously dwells on potential problems and worst-case scenarios. Practice stress reduction techniques such as deep breathing, mindfulness meditation, physical exercise, or engaging in activities you enjoy to help calm your mind and reduce anxiety.

Overthinking often pulls you away from the present moment, causing you to miss out on the joys and experiences happening right now. Engage in mindfulness exercises to bring your attention back to the present. Focus on your senses and immerse yourself in the current experience, whether it's through meditation, mindful eating, or simply observing your surroundings.

Overthinking can lead to indecisiveness, and even after making a decision, you may continue to second-guess yourself and feel regret.

Understand that making mistakes is a natural part of life, and instead of dwelling on regrets, focus on learning from the outcomes of your decisions. Embrace the idea that every decision provides an opportunity for growth.

Overthinking can negatively impact relationships, as excessive analysis can create misunderstandings and strain communication. Practice open and honest communication with your loved ones.

Express your concerns and thoughts, but also actively listen to their perspectives. Trust and respect the perspectives of others, and avoid jumping to conclusions without proper evidence.

To stop overthinking, it's important to cultivate self-awareness and develop strategies that work best for you.

Remember that you have the power to control your thoughts and redirect your focus.

If you find that overthinking is significantly impacting your daily life and causing distress, consider seeking support from a mental health professional who can provide additional guidance and tools tailored to your specific situation.

We can't remain steadfast without hope. But when we cling to hope, we believe that our reward will be worth it.

As I pen down these thoughts, I'm reminded of a teacher who once proposed that perhaps we shouldn't cling to hope. Embracing hope in every aspect of life sets us up for expectations, and navigating through life without expectations might be a simpler path. Absence of expectations means no vulnerability to disappointment. It alleviates the burden of yearning for something or someone to fulfill our needs.

But I choose to believe what God says about HOPE

While the word "hope" is not explicitly mentioned in every translation of religious texts, many believers find encouragement and teachings related to hope in various passages.

- Jeremiah 29:11 (NIV): "For I know the plans I have for you, declares the Lord, plans for welfare and not for evil, to give you a future and a hope."
- Romans 15:13 (NIV): "May the God of hope fill you with all joy and peace as you trust in him, so that you may overflow with hope by the power of the Holy Spirit."
- Psalm 39:7 (NIV): "But now, Lord, what do I look for? My hope is in you."

These verses, among others, reflect the idea that putting trust and hope in God can bring comfort, assurance, and a sense of purpose.

Believers often find solace in the belief that God has good plans for their lives and that having hope in Him leads to a fulfilling and purposeful existence. It's always essential to explore these teachings in the context of one's own faith and beliefs.

However, our infinite minds can't fully comprehend what awaits those who find not just strength but JOY!

What is joy, exactly? It's defined as a feeling of great pleasure or happiness, a sense of thankfulness and gratitude for the small things that come from success, a sense of well-being, or good fortune.

In my perspective, joy is the feeling you work toward despite everything that surrounds you. It's the gratitude for the small things, like sitting outside and hearing the birds, the geese flying over the lake, the wind whistling through the trees, the dove cooing in the distance—these sounds of life bring joy and peace.

Joy in your spirit is the bedrock, influencing your outlook and perspective. Realizing that there is nothing that will happen to you from which you can't glean value, a lesson, a perspective, a quality, or a new lease on life.

I've often been told that I have a light, something about me that draws others to me. I now understand that this "something" my energy, my vibration.

Everywhere I go, people look at me, want to know me, for no apparent reason.

CHAPTER 15

Vibration and
Energy

One's vibrational energy can be like the sun, drawing people in—those who need to have your words, kindness, or joy cast upon them. It can help deliver them from their internal bondage, setting them on a higher plane.

God has placed something special in each of us, a gift, and it's our job to discover that gift.

I believe that one's vibrational energy, the illumination you emit, is felt by others. They want to get to know me, but they don't know why.

The concepts of "vibration" and "energy" are often used in a more metaphorical or spiritual sense rather than in a strictly scientific one.

In various spiritual and metaphysical traditions, these terms are employed to describe the overall state or essence of an individual, encompassing their emotional, mental, and spiritual well-being. Vibration:

- In spiritual or metaphysical terms, "vibration" refers to the energy frequency at which a person operates. It suggests the overall quality of a person's thoughts, emotions, and spiritual alignment. A higher vibration is often associated with positive emotions, love, compassion, and spiritual awareness, while a lower vibration may be linked to fear, negativity, and lower states of consciousness.

Energy:

- "Energy" in this context doesn't refer to the physical energy measured in joules but rather to a more abstract life force or spiritual energy. It's often thought of as the vitality that sustains an individual. Positive energy is associated with feelings of joy, love, and vitality, while negative energy might be linked to stress, fear, and other draining emotions.

Law of Attraction:

- Some spiritual teachings, such as the Law of Attraction, suggest that our thoughts and emotions emit a certain vibrational frequency that attracts similar energies from the universe. Positive thoughts and feelings supposedly attract positive experiences, and vice versa.

Aura:

- The idea of a person's energy is sometimes related to the concept of an aura—a subtle, luminous radiation or field of energy that is said to surround a person. The colors and intensity of the aura are believed to reflect various aspects of a person's emotional and spiritual state.

Holistic Well-Being:

- When people talk about someone's "vibe" or "energy," they may be referring to the overall impression or feeling they get from that person. It could be a combination of body language, facial expressions, emotional demeanor, and the general atmosphere they create.

Spiritual Alignment:

- The terms vibration and energy are often used to describe one's spiritual alignment or connection to higher consciousness. Practices like meditation, prayer, or mindfulness are thought to elevate one's vibration by promoting a sense of inner peace and spiritual awareness.

It's important to note that these concepts are not scientifically proven, and their interpretations can vary widely among different spiritual or metaphysical belief systems.

People may use these terms to express their subjective experiences, beliefs, or intuitive perceptions about the nature of human existence and consciousness.

I believe God has placed me in situations where I didn't belong, granted me access to places I would never have reached on my own, and put me in rooms for which I didn't have the key.

He has whispered my name in people's ears and etched it in their hearts, compelling them to want to bless me. My name lingers in their minds.

I repeat this affirmation every day.

They don't know why, but HE does. They don't know why they are compelled to know me, help me, talk to me, engage with me.

Animals are drawn to me; as I sit here, a mockingbird is perched, just staring at me. Butterflies are usually always around me, landing on me. The other day, a butterfly wouldn't leave me alone! It sat on my fingers for so long that I had to blow it away.

It's our vibration that animals and people pick up on. We attract the same energy level. I can tell when I'm around someone with a low vibration. It's not that they are bad; it's that one vibration level attracts the same level, like a magnet.

I believe that God sends us signs—signs of His presence, signs from our angels—letting us know that we are never alone.

It's our job to be so in tune with ourselves and our surroundings that we recognize these signs. Once we begin to develop these senses, there will never be a time when we can't recognize them.

I have found that the more I stay in tune with the divine, the more my spirit soars to new levels, and the abilities to be captivated and captured by the unimaginable.

Being thankful and grateful with constant praise in my spirit and soul. That's the power of praise.

CHAPTER 16

Self Talk

What you think about yourself is crucial!

Take time to compliment yourself every day. We often spend too much time criticizing ourselves, being our own worst enemy. The pursuit of perfection in ourselves and others prevents us from accepting ourselves and others as they are.

Start acknowledging how far you've come, recognize your strength, and appreciate your talents. Before bedtime, express gratitude to God for creating you with unique and gifted talents. Pray for guidance to discover and develop these talents for the greater good.

Never speak negatively about yourself, either to yourself or others.

Negative self-talk can significantly impact self-esteem and self-worth, reinforcing negative beliefs and diminishing confidence. Positive self-talk, on the other hand, can build a healthy self-image and improve mental and emotional well-being.

Consider the following areas affected by self-talk:

- Self-esteem and self-worth: Negative self-talk diminishes confidence and self-respect. Positive self-talk builds a healthy self-image.

- Perception and mindset: Negative self-talk influences how others perceive and treat us. It can reinforce a pessimistic mindset, limiting personal growth.
- Emotional well-being: Self-deprecating talk reinforces negative emotions, while self-compassion and positive self-talk contribute to emotional well-being.
- Relationships and support systems: Constant self-criticism can impact relationships, while positive self-talk fosters healthier connections.
- Achieving goals: Negative self-talk can be a self-fulfilling prophecy, leading to decreased motivation. Positive self-talk fuels motivation, perseverance, and belief in one's abilities.

Remember, be kind and compassionate to yourself. Acknowledge areas for improvement while balancing self-reflection with self-acceptance, focusing on personal growth rather than self-deprecation.

Words have the power to heal or harm. Ask for guidance to speak words that pierce someone's soul positively.

Learn to lighten up, master your mind, and control your thoughts. Embrace mistakes; they are inevitable. God can guide you to get your mind right physically and mentally.

Create a "to box," a cardboard box with a lid. Write down your feelings, hurts, and pains on pieces of paper, place them in the box, and visualize giving it to God and the universe.

What you give will come back to you, pressed down, shaken together, and running over (Luke 6:38).

Spread positivity by doing good, smiling, conversing, and laughing. Be light-hearted, joyous, and upbeat—it's contagious.

Speak blessings over yourself:

May I be filled with joy and gratitude, appreciating the beauty and abundance in my life. May I have the strength and courage to overcome any challenges that come my way. May I be surrounded by love and support, and may my relationships be filled with understanding and compassion.

May I have clarity of mind and wisdom to make wise decisions. May I be open to new opportunities and experiences, and may they bring growth and fulfillment to my life.

May I be healthy and strong, both in body and mind, and may I take care of myself with love and compassion.

May I be successful in my endeavors and achieve my goals. May my work be meaningful and fulfilling, positively impacting the lives of others. May I continue to learn and grow, expanding my knowledge and skills.

May I have peace and inner harmony, finding balance in all aspects of my life. May I be resilient and adaptable, embracing change and learning from it. May I live with purpose and passion, making a positive difference in the world around me.

I embrace these blessings and affirmations for myself. May they manifest in my life and bring forth abundance, joy, and fulfillment.

Remember, God will cause people to bless and prosper you right in front of those who used you and tried to cause you harm.

Throughout the day, especially at night, speak blessings over yourself and your loved ones. Extend blessings even to those who have hurt you. Affirm that God's mercy and goodness will follow you. Speak of supernatural blessings and favor, trusting that God will chase you down.

Deuteronomy 28:2 declares that God's blessings will chase after you and overtake you. Recognize that God is the Good Shepherd, as depicted in Matthew 18 and Luke 15. He leaves the 99 to search for the one that has wandered away. Your worth to God is immeasurable, and finding you brings Him immense joy.

CHAPTER 1 7

Find Your
Unique Gift

Serving others is my gift.

I have been teaching fitness classes for years. It's essential to me to share my experiences with health and fitness, especially with seniors, enabling them to enjoy the quality of life as they age and undergo changes—not only physically but socially and mentally.

During my classes, I maintain an upbeat atmosphere, incorporating humor and avoiding excessive seriousness. Seniors often join for the social aspect, seeking the joyous atmosphere and camaraderie.

Our elderly population is vulnerable. Some have lost spouses or live alone, enduring days without visitors.

They may experience feelings of loneliness and depression. Providing them with a place to be themselves, surrounded by others, instills hope and contentment.

I've been told that without these exercise classes, many wouldn't have the quality of life or coping mechanisms to endure their hardships.

Incorporating oldies music and laughter, I foster positivity while encouraging them to do their best.

Life isn't meant to be humdrum—a mere attempt to get by. It should be a life filled with joy, happiness, wealth, health, positivity, and caring.

I believe our purpose on Earth is to help others, to be kind, caring, and to serve where God places us.

True understanding comes from feeling what others feel—compassion.

Now, I understand in my heart that everyone has a story, experiences from which others can draw lessons. We need to be willing to feel the hurt, get through it, learn from it, and then share it with a needing, hurting world. It's crucial to learn from our experiences without bitterness.

Many carry hurt, resentment, bitterness, and unforgiveness in their hearts, unable to let go. They may fear that releasing this pain will leave an uncomfortable void. It's like holding onto venom that, if released, could bring discomfort and uncertainty.

Not letting go of past hurts can become a destructive force, much like keeping venom inside. You can observe it in people's faces—sadness, a lack of joy and peace. Sometimes, these individuals are the ones we find challenging to love.

Yet, they are the ones God calls us to love the most.

It's easy to love those who are joyful and light-hearted, but we are also called to reach out to the broken-hearted and seemingly "unlovable."

Some individuals cling to victimhood, carrying past hurts as a sense of purpose, not realizing that it's what may be destroying them. In the fitness industry, negativity has been linked to sickness and disease.

I've heard stories of cancer patients talking to their bodies, declaring the creation of red blood cells or healthy tissue. Studies have shown that this positive affirmation can have a beneficial impact.

CHAPTER 18

The Power Of Words

Power resides in our words—the words we speak to ourselves and about ourselves.

Words are potent tools, capable of inspiring, motivating, comforting, educating, and uniting people. Simultaneously, they can hurt, divide, discourage, and destroy.

The potency of words lies in their ability to evoke emotions, convey ideas, and create connections.

They can express love, gratitude, admiration, giving courage to overcome challenges, inspiring others to be their best selves. Conversely, words can express anger, hate, prejudice, bully, intimidate, and spread false information.

Our choice in using words profoundly impacts those around us. Words shape our beliefs, attitudes, behaviors, influencing the course of our lives. It is crucial to use words wisely, responsibly, choosing them thoughtfully, considering their potential impact on others.

The power of words extends beyond verbal communication. Written words, found in books, articles, and social media posts, significantly impact people's lives.

The written word spreads ideas, knowledge, inspiration, connecting people across great distances and time periods.

God likened the tongue (your words) to a small organ but powerful, like a ship's rudder controlling the entire vessel. Similar to the snake analogy, words can heal or hurt. They act as a potent poison, affecting the whole body, cutting like a knife to our souls—wounds that are unseen.

Controlling our tongues and using them for good to heal ourselves and others is our purpose. The words we put into the universe always come back to us. Speaking positively over ourselves and pouring positivity into others is essential.

Writing about mistakes and faults, if it helps even one person, brings great joy and fulfills the intended purpose.

Addressing the fear of judgment, questioning what others might think, is a significant hurdle.

Reflecting on why events happened, our contribution, and conscious thought about outcomes are crucial aspects.

Recognizing repeated patterns and consciously deciding to change them is a vital part of the learning process.

The realization that living purposefully is more important than taking oneself too seriously brings a shift in perspective.

While we may fool others, we can't fool God. He knows our heart and our intentions—the significant aspect being our intentions.

CHAPTER 19

Intentions

The spiritual significance of the word "intention" is closely tied to the power of consciousness, focus, and purpose in shaping our reality and guiding our actions.

In various spiritual and philosophical traditions, intention is seen as a fundamental force that drives our thoughts, emotions, and behaviors, ultimately influencing the course of our lives and the energy we attract.

- Manifestation: Intention is often considered a key element in the process of manifestation. When we set clear and positive intentions, we align ourselves with the universe's creative energy, and this alignment can lead to the realization of our desires and goals.

- Conscious Creation: In spiritual practices, intention is linked to conscious creation. By being aware of our intentions, we take responsibility for the energy we project into the world, and this mindfulness can lead to more positive and harmonious outcomes.

- Alignment with Higher Self: Setting pure and authentic intentions can be a way of aligning with our higher self or soul. When we act from a place of deep inner truth, our actions become more in line with our spiritual purpose.

- Mindfulness and Presence: Intention encourages us to be present and mindful in our thoughts and actions. By cultivating focused intention, we can let go of distractions and connect more deeply with the present moment.

- Connection with Divine or Source: Intention can also be seen as a way to communicate with the divine or the source of all creation. By setting intentions, we open ourselves up to higher guidance and surrender to a greater plan.

- Healing and Transformation: In spiritual healing practices, intention plays a significant role. By directing positive intentions towards ourselves or others, we can facilitate healing and transformation on emotional, mental, and even physical levels.

- Service and Compassion: Setting intentions that are based on serving the greater good and showing compassion towards others can elevate our spiritual journey and help create a more harmonious world.

- Gratitude and Surrender: Gratitude is often intertwined with intention. Expressing gratitude for what we have and the intentions we set can amplify the positive energy and open us up to receiving more blessings.

Intentions play a crucial role in relationships, influencing the dynamics, quality, and longevity of the connection between individuals. Here's an explanation of why intentions are important in relationships:

Clarity of Purpose:

- Intentions provide a clear sense of purpose and direction in a relationship. When both partners understand each other's intentions, they can work together towards common goals, fostering a sense of unity and shared vision.

Alignment of Values:

- Intentions often reflect personal values. When individuals enter a relationship with aligned intentions and values, there is a higher likelihood of harmony and compatibility. Shared values form a solid foundation for a lasting connection.

Communication:

- Expressing intentions involves effective communication. Openly discussing intentions helps in understanding each other's needs, expectations, and long-term plans. This communication creates transparency and trust within the relationship.

Building Trust:

- Consistent and genuine intentions contribute to building trust. When individuals can rely on each other to act in ways that align with their stated intentions, it establishes a sense of security and reliability in the relationship.

Conflict Resolution:

- Understanding each other's intentions provides valuable insights during conflicts. Misunderstandings can often be resolved by referring back to the original intentions and finding common ground based on shared objectives.

Emotional Safety:
- Clear intentions create an emotionally safe environment. When individuals feel secure in knowing what to expect from each other, it reduces anxiety and allows for a deeper emotional connection.

Long-Term Commitment:
- Intentions are a key factor in long-term commitment. Knowing that both partners are committed to similar life goals and values strengthens the foundation of the relationship and promotes its endurance.

Personal Growth:
- Intentions can be growth-oriented. In a relationship with growth-focused intentions, individuals support each other's personal development, creating a positive and nurturing environment.

Shared Responsibility:
- Intentions involve a commitment to shared responsibilities. Whether it's in managing daily tasks or making significant life decisions, having aligned intentions encourages both partners to actively contribute to the relationship.

Creating a Positive Atmosphere:
- Positive intentions contribute to a positive atmosphere within the relationship. When individuals approach the relationship with love, kindness, and support, it fosters an environment that promotes happiness and fulfillment.

In summary, intentions serve as a roadmap for a relationship, guiding the behaviors, decisions, and overall direction of the connection between individuals. Understanding and aligning intentions contribute significantly to the success and satisfaction within a relationship.

Overall, the spiritual meaning of intention revolves around the idea that our thoughts, feelings, and actions are interconnected and have the potential to influence our reality and the world around us.

By understanding and harnessing the power of intention, we can consciously participate in the unfolding of our lives and align ourselves with higher principles of love, compassion, and purpose.

We can act a certain way for others, but they don't know our heart. God sees all! He sees our intentions and knows what we have in our minds and thoughts and in our heart.

Nothing or no one is hidden. Things that are done in darkness will eventually be brought to light.

Put those whom have hurt you, into God's hands. He is the ultimate judge and vindicator

If we attempt to judge, that means we are still carrying poisonous venom inside.

God and the universe are all-knowing, omnipotent, ever-present in our lives. In times of trouble, God lifts us up with His right hand, placing our feet on a rock.

By releasing and praying, genuinely praying for that person, you are freeing yourself from the pain. It doesn't mean that you are saying that their actions were right; absolutely not!

It's the snake scenario again, releasing the venom so that your life is pure from malice and bitterness.

Freedom

The phrase "live and let live" comes to mind. We are meant to mind our own business and not interfere in others' lives.

On the other hand, recognizing a need and summoning the courage to step in and offer assistance when led by God is the tricky part.

Leaning on our intuition and prayer can help us discern many things. The spirit can guide and warn us; we just have to be tuned in to His voice and guidance.

Sunflowers

I enjoy drawing parallels between humans and other elements in God's creation.

It seems like He blended aspects of all created things together.

The sunflower holds spiritual significance for many. Its resemblance to the sun and its perpetual quest for light make it a symbol of loyalty, happiness, optimism, honesty, peace, admiration, and devotion.

Sunflowers always turn their faces toward the sun, from morning to evening, akin to humans looking to God or their spiritual guide.

Sunflowers literally focus on the bright side. Humans, like sunflowers, operate on a circadian rhythm, an internal clock following a 24-hour cycle. Just like sunflowers are naturally drawn to the sun, humans are drawn to the light.

It's a testament to how God's influence is present in everything.

If we can find goodness in all things, we can find goodness in each and every person. Cultivating an attitude of happiness, radiating light, not only aids in our own healing but also contributes to healing others by drawing them closer to us.

By focusing our minds on something other than ourselves and pouring into others, we experience healing.

There are ways to give advice , if someone asks

When writing this book , I pondered how I would give my relationship advice if someone asks. Knowing how, when or if is the crucial question.

Giving Unsolicited Advice

It's wise to exercise caution when offering unsolicited advice, and even when it's requested, certain considerations should be kept in mind.

Relevance

First and foremost, ensure that your advice is pertinent to the situation. Take into account the context, the individual's needs, and the specific issue they are dealing with.

Expertise

Consider your level of expertise or experience in the given area. If you possess relevant knowledge, your advice may carry more weight.

However, it's crucial to be honest about your qualifications and recognize your limitations.

Permission

Before offering advice, make sure you have the person's permission to do so. Unsolicited advice may not be well-received and can be perceived as intrusive or judgmental. If the person has explicitly asked for advice or has indicated a willingness to receive it, proceed accordingly.

Empathy and Understanding

Approach the situation with empathy. Seek to understand the person's perspective by actively listening and asking clarifying questions.

Empathizing with their feelings and experiences can enhance the thoughtfulness and effectiveness of your guidance.

Respectful Communication

Your approach is vital. Communicate your advice in a respectful and non- judgmental manner. Acknowledge that your advice represents just one perspective, and the individual may choose to accept or reject it. Frame your suggestions as options rather than imposing your views.

In conclusion, the decision to offer advice should be based on the situation, your relationship with the person, and your level of expertise.

Approach advice-giving with humility, recognizing the uniqueness of everyone's circumstances and perspectives.

These are the lessons I've learned from heartbreak and a broken spirit.

Experiencing profound pain has led to a rebirth of my former self. No more self-pity or questioning why these hardships occurred;

now, it's about expressing gratitude to God for caring enough to discipline me.

Much like disciplining a child, the pain hurts the disciplinarian more than the disciplined. Without discipline, rebellion and a lack of respect for oneself and others can result.

Heartbreak, pain, sadness, and loss are pathways to understanding and enjoying the rewards of life.

I'm gradually learning to love myself and becoming comfortable with solitude. Being alone doesn't equate to loneliness. Some individuals embrace solitude as a means of introspection, fostering creativity, or promoting personal growth.

Loneliness, on the other hand, can persist even in the company of others, stemming from a lack of deep emotional connections or a sense of belonging.

It's a complex emotional experience influenced by individual traits, social dynamics, and life circumstances.

Loneliness can arise from various situations, such as moving to a new place, experiencing loss, or going through significant life transitions. While being alone doesn't guarantee loneliness, it's crucial to address feelings of loneliness when they emerge, as social connection and support are vital for overall well-being.

This journey is providing me with a new perspective on life, and I want to share my insights with others, offering them a glimpse into my experiences.

Avoiding Self Judgement

Avoiding self-judgment is challenging but achievable through practice and self-compassion, fostering a more accepting and non-judgmental attitude toward oneself.

Here are some strategies to stop judging yourself:

- Pay attention to your thoughts and emotions:

    Observe your thoughts and emotions without immediate judgment. Recognize moments of self-criticism and consciously choose to release those judgments.

- Challenge your inner critic:

    Question the validity of negative self-judgments. Explore whether there is evidence supporting these judgments or if they stem from assumptions or self-imposed expectations. Replace self-criticism with realistic and compassionate self-talk.

- Practice self-compassion:

    Treat yourself with the kindness and understanding you would extend to a friend in a similar situation. Acknowledge that making mistakes and experiencing imperfections is a part of being human. Use self- compassionate language and engage in self-care activities.

- Adopt a growth mindset:

    Focus on growth and learning rather than fixed judgments about your abilities or worth. View failures and setbacks as opportunities for development rather than indications of personal shortcomings.

- Focus on strengths and progress:

    Shift your attention to your strengths, accomplishments, and progress instead of dwelling on perceived flaws or failures. Celebrate small achievements and milestones along the way.

    Avoid unrealistically high standards: Set challenging yet attainable goals, allowing room for mistakes and learning. Avoid imposing unrealistically high standards on yourself.

- Surround yourself with positive influences:

    Spend time with people who uplift and support you, appreciating you for who you are. Limit exposure to toxic or judgmental individuals who bring you down.

- Practice mindfulness and self-reflection:

    Engage in mindfulness or meditation practices to develop a non- judgmental awareness of the present moment. Regular self-reflection can provide insights into your patterns of self-judgment, allowing you to take steps to change them.

Remember, self-acceptance and self-compassion are ongoing practices that require patience and persistence. Be kind to yourself throughout the process and celebrate your progress along the way.

Every circumstance has a purpose, and acknowledging it with courage brings the promise of a reward. Being brave doesn't mean the absence of fear but walking through circumstances in spite of fear.

Your attitude is the vehicle that will either propel or deter you, and I'm here to assure you that navigating with a positive attitude can lead to significant progress.

Don't Take Things Personally: A Guide to Emotional Resilience

Taking things personally is a common human tendency, often leading to unnecessary stress and conflict. Here's why it's beneficial not to take things personally:

- Recognize the Source: People's words or actions usually reflect their own thoughts, emotions, and experiences, not necessarily about you. Understanding this can help you detach from unnecessary conflicts.
- Build Self-Worth: Develop a strong sense of self and self-worth. When you have a healthy level of self-esteem, external opinions or criticism have less impact.
- Practice Empathy: Put yourself in the other person's shoes.

Recognize that hurtful behavior might stem from their insecurities or personal struggles. Responding with compassion can diffuse potential conflicts.

- Choose Your Battles: Not every comment or action requires a personal response. Evaluate the source, intention, and relevance of feedback before deciding its significance.
- Emotional Resilience: Detach from negative emotions and remind yourself of your control over reactions. Take a step back, breathe deeply, and process your emotions before responding.

- Adopt a Growth Mindset: View criticism as an opportunity for growth rather than a personal attack. Use constructive feedback to enhance your skills and abilities.
- Positive Self-Talk: Develop positive affirmations to reinforce your strengths and accomplishments regularly. Building a positive self- image reduces the impact of negative comments.

Remember, not taking things personally is a skill that takes time and practice. It's about choosing how to respond to situations while maintaining a healthy perspective on yourself and others. This approach cultivates better relationships, reduces stress, and enhances overall well- being.

In our life experiences, we have a helper guiding us, whether we acknowledge it or not. Relying solely on oneself can lead to irrational choices based on upbringing, modeled behaviors, or fleeting emotions. Being aware of the power of words, particularly our self-talk, is crucial. Our thoughts guide us, and whatever we think, we become.

Acknowledging negative thoughts and immediately shutting them down empowers us to control our minds.

We can break free from negative thought pattern, not believing everything that comes into our minds. Instead, we can consciously choose positive thoughts, turning them into actions that shape our lives positively.

Lastly, making assumptions can lead to misunderstandings or biased judgments. Open communication and seeking clarification are better alternatives to assumptions, preventing unnecessary conflicts and fostering understanding

CHAPTER 21

Assumptions

Remember that making assumptions can lead to misunderstandings or biased judgments. It's often better to seek clarification and engage in open communication to avoid unnecessary conflicts or confusion.

Don't make assumptions

Making assumptions in relationships can be detrimental because it often leads to misunderstandings, miscommunications, and unnecessary conflicts.

Here's how assumptions can cause harm:

- Misunderstandings: Assumptions are based on interpretations, and these interpretations might not always align with the actual intentions or thoughts of the other person. This can lead to misunderstandings where both parties have different perceptions of a situation.

- Unrealistic Expectations: Assumptions can create unrealistic expectations. When we assume we know what someone else is thinking or feeling without clear communication, we set ourselves up for disappointment if our assumptions turn out to be incorrect.

- Communication Breakdown: Assuming we know what the other person means or wants without verifying can lead to a breakdown in communication. This lack of clarity can result in conflicts and a failure to address important issues.

- . Conflict and Resentment: Unchecked assumptions may lead to conflicts based on incorrect information. Over time, if assumptions are not addressed, they can build up and create resentment in the relationship.

To avoid making assumptions and foster healthier relationships:

- Practice Active Listening: Pay close attention to what the other person is saying, and ask clarifying questions to ensure you understand their perspective correctly.

- Seek Clarification: If something is unclear or if you're making assumptions, ask the other person for clarification. It's better to confirm than to assume.

- Express Yourself Clearly: Clearly communicate your thoughts, feelings, and expectations to avoid leaving room for misinterpretation. Be open and honest about your needs and concerns.

- Avoid Mind Reading: Don't assume you know what someone else is thinking or feeling. Instead, ask them directly and encourage open communication.

- Practice Empathy: Try to see situations from the other person's perspective. This can help you understand their intentions and feelings better, reducing the likelihood of making inaccurate assumptions.

- Question Your Assumptions: Before acting on an assumption, question its validity. Consider alternative interpretations and recognize that your assumptions may not always reflect reality.
- Create a Culture of Open Communication: Foster an environment where open and honest communication is encouraged. This allows both parties to express themselves without fear of judgment.

By actively working to avoid assumptions and promoting clear communication, you can build trust, understanding, and stronger connections in your relationships.

I want girls and women to understand that their self-worth is more precious than jewels, rubies, and gold. For many, self-esteem wasn't instilled during their upbringing.

The search for validation leads us to compromise, offering our time, value, and everything to someone without them earning the right to be in our presence.

Would you willingly give up your jewels, your money to someone who exploits you for their pleasure and gain? Someone uninterested in your worth, feelings, or genuine love and adoration. Someone who doesn't even value themselves, let alone you? No!

At 66, I sometimes feel like I've wasted my years, now on the downside of life. But God promises restoration, to give back what the locusts have eaten. Regardless of why it happened, He will transform us, making beauty from our ashes, akin to the Japanese art of kintsugi. We become more valuable than in the beginning.

Guard your heart against negativity and thoughts not for your higher good. Proverbs 4:23 advises us to do so, for it determines the course of our lives.

Listen to your inner voice.

Ignoring your inner voice and neglecting red flags can have significant consequences.

In cases where children are involved, it can impact them, leading to physical and psychological harm.

I experienced a toxic relationship that escalated to the point where my partner not only controlled me but also my children. The abuse became visible, with him tearing my clothes off in front of them. This should have been a clear signal to end it.

Domestic violence often starts subtly, with name-calling, and gradually intensifies to physical harm. It may begin with a push, a poke, then escalate to more severe actions like slapping or choking.

Living with regrets about allowing such behavior haunted me for years.

Children, however, always remember, and my gratitude goes to God that mine have grown into loving, respectful, and productive adults.

We all make mistakes, and only Jesus was perfect. Therefore, I pray and thank the Lord for guiding my steps each day.

Exercise caution if you sense something off about someone, even those close to you.

Online dating, as I discovered, can be challenging. The advice I received was to treat it like regular dating, recognizing that among many, you'll find that one ideal partner.

However, instincts play a crucial role. If something feels wrong or raises doubts, listen to that inner voice.

I've learned not to give the benefit of the doubt. Trust your instincts from the beginning; if it feels wrong, it probably is. Don't let your heart override your instincts.

Being vigilant is crucial. If someone avoids video chatting, they may have something to hide. If they're uncomfortable being seen, it's a red flag.

Insecurity about appearance is not something you want in a partner. Additionally, if two weeks pass without the prospect of a date, it's time to move on. I encountered a situation where a guy left on a supposed business trip two days before our scheduled date, extending his absence with unconvincing reasons.

Exclusivity

Your exclusivity is a prize that must be earned.

The decision to give or withhold the gift of exclusivity in a relationship is a personal one that depends on several factors.

Here are some considerations for when to give or not give your gift of exclusivity to someone:

When to give your gift of exclusivity:

Mutual feelings: If you and your partner have developed a strong emotional connection and both express a desire for exclusivity, it may be the right time to give your gift of exclusivity.

Shared values and goals: If you and your partner align on important values and share common long-term goals, it can be a good indication that you're ready to commit exclusively to each other.

Trust and communication: Open and honest communication is vital in any relationship. If you and your partner have established a foundation of trust and effective communication, it can provide a solid basis for offering exclusivity.

Emotional readiness: Consider whether you are emotionally ready for a committed relationship and whether you genuinely desire a deeper level of intimacy and exclusivity with your partner.

When not to give your gift of exclusivity:

Uncertain or incompatible feelings: If you're unsure about your feelings for the person or you have doubts about your compatibility, it might be wise to hold off on offering exclusivity until you have a clearer understanding.

Lack of trust or communication issues: If there are ongoing trust issues or difficulties in communication that haven't been adequately addressed, it's important to work on those before considering exclusivity.

Different relationship expectations: If you and your partner have differing expectations for the nature and pace of the relationship, it's crucial to have a conversation and ensure you're on the same page before moving forward with exclusivity.

Recent breakup or emotional baggage: If either you or your partner has recently ended a significant relationship or carries emotional baggage that could impact the new relationship, it might be best to allow more time to heal and establish emotional stability before committing to exclusivity.

Ultimately, the decision to offer exclusivity should be based on your personal judgment and the unique dynamics of your relationship.

It's essential to communicate openly with your partner, be honest about your feelings, and consider what feels right for both of you

Embracing Wholeness

As I sit here, reflecting on the journey that brought me from the depths of heartbreak to the shores of self-love, I can't help but feel an overwhelming sense of gratitude.

The path was not an easy one, but every step, every tear shed, and every moment of despair was a necessary part of my transformation. I have finally unlocked the key to self-love, and I am ready to share it with the world.

In the aftermath of heartbreak, I found myself at a crossroads. I could either allow my pain to define me, to consume me entirely, or I could choose to rise above it, to discover the true essence of who I am. I made the courageous decision to embark on a journey of self-discovery, a journey that would lead me to the most profound love of all – the love for myself.

The first step was acknowledging and embracing my pain. I allowed myself to grieve, to feel the depth of my emotions, and to honor the loss I had experienced. In doing so, I realized that my heartbreak was not a reflection of my worthiness or my ability to love. It was simply a part of my story, a chapter that had come to an end. By accepting this truth, I began to release the grip it had on my soul.

With newfound clarity, I turned my attention inward. I delved into the depths of my being, exploring the layers of my identity that had been overshadowed by my past relationships.

I reconnected with my passions, my dreams, and the unique qualities that make me who I am. I embraced my flaws and imperfections, recognizing that they are what make me beautifully human.

Self-care became my compass on this journey. I prioritized my physical, emotional, and spiritual well-being. I nourished my body with wholesome food, engaged in activities that brought me joy, and surrounded myself with positive influences. I learned to listen to my inner voice, to trust my intuition, and to set boundaries that protected my heart.

In the process of self-discovery, I unearthed wounds that had long been buried. I faced my fears head-on, confronting the limiting beliefs and negative self-talk that had held me back for far too long. It was not an easy task, but with each wound I healed, I grew stronger and more resilient.

As I cultivated self-love, I began to attract healthier relationships into my life. I surrounded myself with individuals who celebrated my journey, who saw my worth, and who uplifted me in ways I had never experienced before.

I learned that true love starts from within and radiates outward, attracting those who appreciate and honor the love we have for ourselves.

Now, as I stand at the precipice of wholeness, I am filled with an unshakeable sense of peace and love. I understand that self-love is not a destination; it is a lifelong commitment. It requires daily practice, self- compassion, and forgiveness. It is a continuous journey of growth and self-discovery.

I share my story not as a final chapter but as a new beginning, a testament to the power of the human spirit and our innate capacity to heal. If you find yourself lost in the depths of heartbreak, I implore you to have faith in your own resilience. Trust that within you lies the key to unlocking a love so profound that it will illuminate your path and transform your life.

Cracking the Love Code, the journey is a testament to our strength, our resilience, and our ability to rise above the pain.

I encourage you to embark on this transformative journey of self-love, for within it lies the power to heal, to grow, and to embrace the beautiful, whole person you are destined to become.

With an open heart and a renewed sense of purpose, I step forward into the world, ready to share my story and inspire others to unlock their own key to self-love.

May my words serve as a guiding light for those who are ready to embrace their own journey from heartbreak to wholeness.

Remember, dear reader, you are deserving of love, and it all begins with the love you have for yourself. Embrace it, nurture it, and let it guide you on the path to wholeness.

"Sometimes things fall apart, so better things can fall together"
Marilyn Monroe

ABOUT THE AUTHOR

Veta Newton is a remarkable individual who has dedicated her life to empowering women and helping them navigate the intricacies of love, heartbreak, and self-discovery. As a first-time author, she has made an indelible mark on the literary world with her insightful and transformative book, *"Cracking the Love Code: Unveiling the Lessons of Heartbreak and Relationship Mishaps."*

With a wealth of experience in the fitness industry spanning over 35 years, Veta began her career as a fitness specialist. Throughout her journey, she honed her expertise as a nutritionist, health coach, and personal trainer, inspiring countless individuals to adopt healthier lifestyles and transform their well-being.

Her comprehensive understanding of the mind-body connection, coupled with her passion for empowering women, has been instrumental in her success as a sought-after authority in the field.

However, Veta's expertise extends far beyond fitness and nutrition.

Recognizing the profound impact of relationships on overall well-being, she immersed herself in the study of human connection and emotional healing. Through her own personal experiences and extensive research, Veta became an expert in understanding the complexities of heartbreak and the detrimental patterns that often sabotage relationships.

Now, as an accomplished author, Veta shares her invaluable wisdom with women over 40, guiding them on a transformative journey to unravel the complexities of heartbreak and rediscover the power of self-love. In her groundbreaking book, "Cracking the Love Code," she offers a compassionate and insightful roadmap for healing, growth, and finding true fulfillment in relationships.

Veta's unique approach combines practical guidance, psychological insights, and empowering exercises, allowing her readers to transcend their past traumas and embrace a future filled with love, joy, and personal empowerment. Her ability to empathize and connect deeply with her audience has garnered her a loyal following of women seeking guidance and support in navigating the challenges of love and relationships.

Beyond her written work, Veta Newton is a dynamic speaker and a passionate advocate for empowering women. Through workshops, seminars, and one-on-one coaching, she shares her expertise, helping individuals transform their lives and create authentic, fulfilling connections.

With Veta Newton as their guide, women over 40 embark on a transformative journey of self-discovery, gaining the tools and insights necessary to break free from destructive patterns and cultivate lasting love and happiness. Her unwavering commitment to helping others and her wealth of knowledge make her an invaluable resource in the realm of relationships and personal growth.

Veta Newton's mission is to empower women to become the architects of their own love stories, transforming heartbreak into a catalyst for personal evolution and opening the doors to a future filled with love, authenticity, and self-empowerment.

Printed in the USA
CPSIA information can be obtained
at www.ICGtesting.com
LVHW021628020224
770787LV00002B/262